T0078043

Yesterday
to
Present

Brooklyn Bob

authorHOUSE·

AuthorHouse™
1663 Liberty Drive
Bloomington, IN 47403
www.authorhouse.com
Phone: 833-262-8899

Published by AuthorHouse 05/19/2022

ISBN: 978-1-6655-5979-9 (sc)
ISBN: 978-1-6655-5911-9 (e)

Library of Congress Control Number: 2022909196

Print information available on the last page.

Contents

Yesterday to Present

1947 TO 2021

Born in Brooklyn, N.Y. 1947. Grew up in Brooklyn. My mom and dad got married in 1945, they met through friends. My dad was discharged from the Army; after World War Two. I have a sister, she was born in February 1946. My sister told me that I would sit on window sill, and watch the children playing outside. I would sit at the window without by diaper on, I was showing off my private parts. I was a seven month baby. I was different than other boys. I was premature I was four pounds twelve ounces. I was placed in an incubator, until I gain weight of seven pounds. My sister, when she was older, my mom taught my sister to give me a bath. She was giving me a bath all the time.

My mom call her sister up told her to come over and bring Maureen, so Maureen can play with my sister. She would play with my sister, and they both would give me a bath.

My mom sister was my God mother. She knew how I was different from other boys. My mom called her sister told her sister stop by our house. My mom told her sister she is making meat loaf. Don't forget to bring Maureen after school. Maureen was in kindergarten. My sister will play with her cousin. She stood in touch with our cousin Maureen. They both gave me a bath. Maureen didn't have any brothers. She was happy to come over to our house. Hoping it was time for me to get a bath. I guess she liked looking at my private part. My parts are different then hers and my sister. Two years later by mom's sister had a baby boy. My mom's sister brought her son Ricky over. My sister and Maureen would give Ricky a bath. He was a normal boy. A coupler of years later, my aunt gave birth to another girl. They name her Karen. I started going to school when I was five years old.

My sister started first. My sister was thirteen months older than me. Then the following year. We both went to school together we went to Catholic school. Our mom would take both of us. We would walk up the block to Saint Leonard Catholic School. We went to Saint Leonard's Church on Sundays. We was there for two years, my sister got in trouble with the nuns.

So my mother and father took us out of catholic school; and put us into public school. My sister and I played together.

But as I got older we fought among ourselves. In 1954 my father was coming out of work. A friend of him would drive him home. My father got hit by a car, hit and run coming out of work. They say he was toss thirty feet in the air. He worked four pm until midnight. He worked at a stove company. Well-built Stove was the company name, He worked at.

He was taken to Wyckoff hospital. They never caught

the car. Everybody was parked bumper to bumper. So my father's friend had to wait for other driver to move their cars before he would be able to chase or look for that car. My father, he had a compound fracture of his right leg. He was in and out of the hospital three or four times. The doctors needed to check the leg make sure the cast didn't move. He was out of worked for four years. We had to go on welfare. I had to take him everywhere he had to go. I was almost seven years old. This happen February 1954.

My mother had to find work. Because welfare didn't give a lot of money for a family of four. I would miss a lot of time from school. I would be hold back in June. All my friend went into next grade. I was kept in that grade until October. The school would put me in the right grade, they kept me there because I loss a lot of time. One month for my time loss at school. The next year it happen again. This happen for three years. On my days off from school.

I would played in the park, and in the street. I would play stick ball, played with friends, family members. One day while I was walking to school, I kick something. I bent over to pick it up, it was a rusted pair of vise crisp. A couple of days later, I took this vise crisp to Sears. I told the sale man my brother asked me to bring these to sears. I gave it to salesman. He told me to wait, he will be right back. He came back with a new pair. He asked me to sign form. I did and left the store. with a new pair of vise crisp. My father started going fishing.

My father started taking me fishing with him. My father tauch me how to fish. Showed me how to bait the hook. I went fishing with him. Other times we would go with Mom and my sister. My sister and I would walk on

3

the beach. One time I was following her on this big pipe coming into the water coming from across the highway. I slip off fell into water. Where I fell, there was a hole in sand, I fell into it. I remember going down into the hole, water was above my head. I was about eight years old.

Another time walking in parking lot, I found a wallet. Gave wallet to my dad. He took wallet to park office. Park officer, checked address found that woman was fishing. He walk around Canarsie pier. He located that lady. He gave the wallet to a lady who lost it. This lady gave officer two quarters to give to me for finding her wallet. I was happy. I gave the two quarters to my dad. This was in August.

Started school in September. Attended Public School 53, learn to read, and write, and math. Every day after school, did homework, then ate super. Then went outside to play. Had a speech problem. Also I didn't spell well, or read well. This was a problem because I couldn't sound out words right. My sister was my hero, if I got into a fight, she would stop the other boy from beating me up. My dad never taught me to fight. He said fighting wasn't good.

I remember one day there was a very loud noise outside, I went with my friend Raymond to see what the noise was, and where it came from. There was a small restaurant three blocks away. The guy who owe this restaurant. Was selling fireworks. He didn't want the police to know he was selling fireworks. Selling firework is against the law. So he placed the box of fireworks under the stove. The lady who did the cooking, didn't know about the fireworks. As she was cooking a spark fell from the stove into the box. That was the loud noise I heard. The lady eyeballs was hanging from her head. I'll never forget this. The stove flew through two floors, and roof. We stood there for a while. Waited for ambulance to take woman to hospital.

Then Raymond and I went to the park to play hand ball. This was Knickerbocker Park. The park was down the next block. So we walk over. We went to the hand ball court. We got a court. We started to play if anybody wanted to play. They would play against us. If they beaded us then they would have the court. We would play another game. When someone new came to play. If he didn't have a partner one of us would team up with him. We would start a new game. If he had a partner, then we would play for the court. If we won, the court is still ours. If we loss, then the court belongs to them. Then sometimes we would stay or go home.

I started back to school in September of 1959. Is when I went to Jr. High School 162! Learn more education. Learn typing. More math, Graduate in June 1962. Went down the block to get lunch. Purchased a tuna fish sandwich. The tuna fish sandwich was on a hero bread, it cost twenty five cents. The sandwich was very good. Some other times I would meet my father at the diner, he would buy me a hamburger. Back in that day hamburgers was twenty-five cents.

I tried smoking with Raymond, and other kids. The other boys, they indicate if we wanted to hang with us you need to smoke. You see those cartoons on TV showing kids smoking and their faces turning blue. My face, and Raymond face didn't turn blue, but we was very sick.

My mother checked me to see why I wasn't feeling good. I never said anything about trying to smoke. The next day, Raymond and I went down to a knitting mill.

We bought a pack of Robert Burns' typo. Put them into a knitting cone, this cone was made of a heavy cardboard. We try to try to smoke again. Again we got very sick again.

After that day I never tried smoking again. I was about thirteen years old. During school had gym, played dodge ball, basketball. Learn to dance. Girls wanted to make out with boys. I wasn't interested. Girls would go into closet and make out with a boy. One boy told me the girl went down on him. He said he felt good. But she wouldn't stop with him. She would take another boy to the closet. I learn later she was selling drugs.

In winter, I shoveled snow to make some money. Also had snow ball fights. Sometime Raymond would help me shovel snow. We would charge twenty five or fifty cents. Depending how much snow we had to shovel. A lot of times those people would give us a ten cent tip. I would spite whatever I made with Raymond.

In summer played handball. At Knickerbocker park. Also played fights with carpet guns. Also made racecars for racing. Got a wooded milk box, nailed milk box to two by four. And one skate. Spite the skate, got a two by four. Naiedl one part of skate in front by milk box the other skate at end of two my four.

Then start racing down the street Played with other friends. Made wooden guns to shoot linoleum in a diamond shape. Got a piece of wood. One inch by one inch. Shape it as a gun, nail it together. Used another nail at front, placed a rubber bang on nail. Bend that nail, to keep rubber band from coming off. Then take another nail, nail it to other end. Then get diamond shape linoleum. And now where ready for fights. If someone got hit with that diamond shape linoleum. You he would feel the pain.

I was about fourteen years old. Also worked in a grocery store, for a bag of grocery, my mom would come to store, on Saturday to pick up groceries that she needed. I wood stock shelve with can goods. Put milk into refrigerator. Placed bread and cake on racks. I would worked after school, and all day Saturday. This store was Domagk Deli.

Then went to High School in lower Manhattan. Started September 1962. Study Electrical Installation. Study about motors, transformers, bells, wiring. Bending pipe. Studying about a/c (alternate current) electric 120-240, also 240-440 voltage circuit. And d/c (direct current) circuits 600 voltage electrical. Also low voltage Six and twelve volts, this was bell wiring. Learn how to read voltage meter and an ampere meter. Also learn the color code for wires. Black was hot, it carried one hundred and twenty volts. The white wire was the neutral it brought the voltage back. A red wire was also a hot wire. It was used as a switch leg a blue wire is for lighting. The green wire is ground, sometimes a ground wire doesn't have any color. It was bare copper. It was just bare. In low voltage, the white wire is hot and black wire is the neutral. On automobile Red and white is hot and black wire is negative. Auto batteries are twelve voltage. Also studied math, science and other subject. Went there for three years. Graduate in 1965. I was eighteen years old. Sometimes my friend Pat and I didn't feel like going to school.

We would take our school books and put them in the sand box. On every Ell station there was a sand box. This box was fill with sand. The sand was used for in winder. To put sand on the tracks. To stop train from sliding. When the motorman would apply brakes. Working part time in Bo hack, this is a grocery store, wild going to High School. Also still playing hand ball. Played with friends for soda pop. After Graduation. Still played stick ball in street, played hand ball at Knickerbocker Park.

I was looking for worked. I then apply for a job at the World fair. I got this job in The World Fair, in Flushing, N.Y. Cooking for Brass Rails. Brass Rails is a restaurant in lower Manhattan, around Court Street. Making hamburgers and hot dogs. Selling these hamburgers and hot dogs to people who stop by to eat. Also selling soda pop. Coco cola was main brand. Filling there cups with soda and ice.

Then took a position working at night as the inventory manager. The guy who had this position was going back to college. So he told the boss he was leaving. So the manager asked me if I wanted to change from cooking to inventory. He told me I would get a starting pay of two dollars an hour. Instead of eighty five cent an hour. Which was the minimum pay rate. I told him yes.

I had to start work at ten pm until seven am. He would come in around six am. We would talk, I would show him by list. He would take it and then sign it. Then I was able to punch out. And go home. Carlos told me about people coming by after midnight looking for free food. He said never get anything. He said he thinks the boss would send them.

One night a gypsy woman would come by looking for some free food. I told her I don't have anything. I couldn't save or give her anything. I don't know if she was looking to set me up. I told her I didn't have anything. She said she would get me some sex. I said no, she said are you gay. I said no I'm just working to made a few dollars. I told her good bye, I had to get back to work.

I had to check my inventory, to see what we had on hand, and what I needed to order. Then checked what came in. All the orders came in by truck around five am. When the fair closed. The end of December 1965. The boss asked me if I wanted to go to Manhattan and work at main resurant stay are located at 1851 Park Avenue. I said thank but I need work with Electrical. I study electrical Installation in school. Started looking for a job.

I got a letter in the mail. Indicating for me to go to 3413 Park Ave. For an interview with a company who had an opening in the electric field. This company's office was Local three. Number one union in New York. In the electrical field they indicated the opening wasn't not right away. When someone retires, I would be hired as an electrician's helper. I asked when this will take place. The man said it wouldn't matter. They wanted me to work as a bus boy. This job is to bring mail to other offices. I would place into that position, I would have singularity. I didn't take that offer. I wanted to get into electrical field now, today. Not tomorrow. I kept looking. I went to another office, this was electrical local union number # 99, and they offer me a job. Working in Queens at a movie theater with a contractor. Working as an electrician helper. I took this job, I started Monday morning at eight am as electrician's helper. I took two trains to get there. We were changing and replacing electric around. Making this theatre into a bingo hall. When this job was over, this contractor, came from the Bronx. I found out where they was locater. I followed them. I went and continued working for this company in the Bronx. Their name was B and A electric company. I worked there for ten months. Took three trains to get to the Bronx. Left at 6am to get to work by 8 am. Then started going to night school, learning more about wiring. I team up with a fellow. We started installing cables, and hooking up wires. I remember going to a house in upper Manhattan. We had to install a 120 outlet for an air-cond. This outlet was need a window. These woman purchased a window unit. When we finish I asked one of the woman if I can used the bathroom. She said nc, I thought she was joking. I started walking to the bathroom. She said to me where are you going, I said to use your bathroom. She said I told you no. I said I though you was kidding. When we back to office. The boss told me he was firing me. Had to leave there, because local union # 99 said they primitive me a two year man, but B and An Electric. Boss said I wasn't there a year. So I had to leave. The boss fired me.

I went down to the unemployment office. I had to fill out lots of forms. I got them all fill out. Gave them to a lady at the counter. She told me I needed to come back next week. I would fill out more papers, watch a film. Then come back another week later a sign a check. The following week I would receive this check in the mail. I said to the lady you're saying I won't receive a check until four weeks. She said that is right.

I then rip up these papers. I told her I will fine my own work in a week or so. I then left. The union send me to Brooklyn for electrician's helper job, but when that company heard I came from union. They indicated they didn't need any help. Companies think if a man comes from the union, he a rat. He comes to spy on that company. Local #99 send me to another electric company. But they also didn't hire me, because I told them local # 99 send me.

I found a job on my own. With another contractor, In Queens. I was going to my driving school appointment, I'm learning to drive. I had an uncle who said he would teach me. But he never had time. My uncle also he was my God father. He also told me he would teach and take me hunting. Another lie. He taught me how to eat steak, rare. He also got me into drinking beer. He would come over to my dad house on Friday night. We would drink beer, and then we would play cards. My dad and my uncle taught me to played pinochle. Ten cent per hundred points. Double on spades. So Friday nights became card and beer night.

On Wednesday I went to the auto school. I took two buses to get to the school. I saw an electrical shop. I stop by, asked a fellow if they needed any help. This fellow said I needed to call the boss, Dan. He gave me the phone number of company. He told me to call around three pm. I don't believed in calling. So I took the bus, I got to the electrical shop about three pm. I knock on door. Then rang a bell. A man came down the stairs, open door, asked me how he can help me. I told him I stop by this morning. I talked with a fellow about a job. I asked that fellow if they needed any help. He said to me I would need to call you by phone. I told this guy who opened the door, I don't believed in calling. If someone wants something they need to go after it, not by phone. That man said he like my way of thinking and doing. If I can wait for ten or fifteen minutes his foreman will be coming in. I said yes. I sat down. He said how I knew they was looking for help. I told him I was going to take a driving test. I'm trying to get a driving license. Just then the foreman came in. The foreman asked me a lot of questions, and I gave him the correct answers. He then asked me to draw a bell circuit, also asked if I can hook up a three way system. I did that also. He then asked if I can start on Monday at eight am. I said I will be here sharp. I then went home.

Told my mom and dad I found a job. Monday I took a bus to get to work. I left at 7 am to get to the job by eight AM started as an electrician's helper. After six months I was made an electrician. Dan indicted he was making me an electrician. He said that Ernie, his foreman said to him I was very good what I was doing. Dan hired a fellow, his name was Joe. Joe was my helper. Worked with this contractor for 2 years. We did a lot of jobs together. I got a driver licenses. Joe wanted me to meet his sister. I said to Joe not now. I want to get my journeyman licenses. Dan the boss had to let me go, due to union problems. There was a message on his voice mail. It said Dan you need to let this guy Bob go. He hasn't pay union dues for six months. That day my boss asked me if I knew what this was about. I said yes, I told him while I was going to night school for journeyman education I learn that the union office was burnt down. So I decided to stop paying dues. I told Dan that they never did anything for me. He asked me why I didn't say anything too him. I told him, I couldn't because I though. He would let me go. He told me he is Jewish. And Jewish people don't give money away for anything. He told me that every month he pays money to the union for me an others. He said he would never let me go, because I made him money. And I'm very good what I do. I told him I was sorry. I said good bye. And I went home. He called me later that evening. He told me he called a friend he knew who has a none union shop. His friend name is Joe Goldstein. I went to see his friend Joe. First thing Monday morning. Took this job, work there for three months. Business was very slow. I talk with Joe three months later, told him I needed to leave, because business is slow. I wish I could have given him more time. He said it was OK. He was happy I was going to leave. He told me it was costing him a lot of money. He didn't want to let me go, due to his friend Dan. I told him I got a job at Metropolitan Life Insurance Company on Park Ave. In mid-town Manhattan. He said he would give me a letter of recommendation. I told Joe I didn't need it. Joe went and call Jack and Jim into his office. He told them he was laying them off, because business is slow. He then called Harry his other electrician. He told Harry what was happing. They said to Joe what about Bob. Joe said Bob quit. They came out of office and said to me why did you quit. I said business is slow. I can't see Joe keeping me on hand. And losing money. I told them I got and took another job. I'll be working with Metropolitan Life Insurance Company as an electrician helper. In mid-town Manhattan. My job was to replace lighting. Repairs to other electrical item. Replaced switches, outlets. Whatever needed to be replaced? I worked there for one year and six months.

I came home from work one day. A neighbor was

talking to another neighbor. He was saying that they don't have any heat. THIS WAS November, November is a cold month. Sometimes we got snow. Temperatures would go down into low thirty. Sometimes temperature would drop in twenty, or lower. The tennet, a woman who lives upstairs, with her two daughters. The oldest daughter cut an extension cord with a knife. This cause sparks and smoke. The extension was hanging down from light fixture. They used it to play a radio. The Fire department was called out to check the condition of that apartment they turn off the electric meter. The second floor apartment was where Joe's uncle lived. All of the heating and bells and hall lights was on that meter. When the lady walk away, I said to Joe, I know his name. My mom would go there to baby sit his children. I said to Joe, I just got home from work. If you can give me a litter time I will come over and look at the electric. And let you know what I can do. He said yes come over when you can.

About fifteen minutes later I went over there. I met with Joe. Joe and I went down the to the basement, and I check out the electric. I told Joe I can take the heating cable, the light cable and the bell cable off the meter I will removed them from second floor apartment and put all this on his meter. He said that sounds good. We then went back up stairs. He asked when do you (I) think I can do this. I told Joe I can do this now, all I need is go to my truck and get my tools. He said to me he needs to call his uncle. He need to tell his uncle what I can do. And when I can start. Later when I spoke with his uncle's his uncle was on the phone. I talk to his uncle. I told his uncle how much it will cost him. He said please do what you can. Joe will pay whatever you want. And I'll pay Joe. So I went out to my truck and got my tools and some wire nuts some wire, and some cable. So I went back down into basement. After about two hours. I moved the cable around. I got the heat on I got the bells working, and I got the hall lights on. I had Joe call his uncle back, I told his uncle I would come over tomorrow Saturday and see what I can do to the second and third floors. He said that OK. Just do what is nessarsecry. I will pay you whatever. I went there Saturday morning, I had to go to third floor open the floor boards. I had to replace the cable from the bedroom into the next room. I removed old burnt cable. Remove cable from one room to other room. Replaced cable, and I had removed out let box from ceiling. Tape some of wires that the copper was exposed. I came back down the stairs to Joe apartment. Met his wife sister she is a lovely girl. She was watching the rifleman on tv. Three day later Joe took me to his uncle house, His uncle lived in Cypress Hills. His uncle had his wife make some calamari. When she came home, I also met his wife, brother.

About three weeks later, I finally asked Joe's wife sister out. We started dating. Going to movies, visiting her friends, family. She stood with her older sister. She worked at a pen company. I would bring her a sandwich every other day. I purchased at a Jewish restaurant in Queens. She worked from twelve pm unstill nine pm. Her older sister is going to move to Deer Park Long Island. I knew her sister and family, because my mom would baby sit for them. They went out at night a lot. She went to stay with her other sister. Her other sister lived next door. After they moved to Deer Park, Long Island, New York.

Her older sister was a mother of three daughters and one son. Her husband was a furrier. He worked at a company making mink coats. My Nancy She moved next door to her other sister. She stood there for a While. Then she was having problems with her sister. Her sister boyfriend didn't like me. He told his girlfriend. Your sister needs to leave, or he will. So she went to stay with her brother and his girlfriend. Her brother lived next house over in an apartment on the second floor. My Nancy went back to Puerto Rico to visit her family for a couple of weeks. When she lot back. She told me her father, think I'm a great guy. Joe and her dad and I went fishing one night together. He said to her he thinks I'm the guy she going to marry. He was right. Everybody lived In Brooklyn. Her brother's girlfriend like me a lot, she would lay on the sofa and spread her legs wide open. I told my Girlfriend Nancy. I said tell her I'm with you I'm not interested in her. Tell her this in Spanish. I also told Nancy to tell her to go to Nancy's brother. Take him to bed. The next day she went to babysit for her sister in Deer Park Long Island. I was very mad that week. I drove out to Deer Park I went there with a bottle of Johnny Walker Red in my car, for me to drink. When I got there it was around two am. So I didn't want to wake anybody up, so I slept in my car. Nancy's nieces came outside in the morning, and found me sleeping. The girls went into the house, got their mother to come outside. Their mother came out of her house. She knock on my driver door, woke me up. Asked me what I was doing. I told her I was mad with her brother. He kept telling me he doesn't want me to drive out to Deer Park Long Island. Her sister came out of there house. She said to me come inside I'll make coffee. She went there 2 times a month I drove out there to spend the weekend with her and her sister's family. I was very much in loved with Nancy. Then took her home to her brother's apartment. She didn't lived with her sister anymore. So she went to live with her brother. So on November 8, Nancy's brother in-law came to pick her up from her brother apartment to take her to his home in Deer Park Long Island. To baby sit for him and his wife. They was going out Saturday night to a party. Her brother said to me don't go out to spend time with my sister. I told him OK. But that was only a saying. I left that Saturday evening around 6 pm. I drove to Deer Park. I stood there until her sister and husband came home. Before her sister and husband came home, I asked my Nancy, if she wanted to married me. And come lived at my mom and dad in their apartment. I will look for an apartment for us. After where home. She said that was a good idea. When her sister came back from there night out. We went to sleep, we slept in different bed rooms. When we got up in the morning we had breakfast. After breakfast. We said good bye. To her sister, her sister's husband and three nieces and one nephew.

Getting Married

We left got into my car, 1965 Chevy I drove to Elkton, Maryland. Two hundred thirty-eight miles. We found an adjustor. Where we got married. November 12, 1968. Spend three day on a honeymoon. In a hotel in Elkton. Maryland.

Send a telegram to my boss at Metropolitan Life

Insurance Company. Told him I got married. And I'll be back to work on Monday. He said it's great, but when he received the telegram, he through something happen to his sister. His sister was in the hospital. She was very sick. We drove back to Brooklyn. It was a snowy day. I stop at a service station to get gas and have them check my tire. Gas was thirty-two cents a gallon. They put eight gallons of gas. They found a nail in my tire. I think Nancy's brother put it there, so I wouldn't go out to Long Island. We made it back home. My mother and father, was happy to see us.

I told them we were married, showed them our license. I called Metropolitan Life Insurance Company Monday morning. I told them I quit my job with Metropolitan Life Ins. In lower Manhattan. A friend of ours came by he told me and Nancy that her brother was looking for me. He want to fight me because I didn't listen to him. He said he told me not to go to Long Island. I told that friend to tell Nancy's brother he knows where I live. I told him to tell him if he's man enough come see me now, not tomorrow.

Don't come drunk. About an hour later he came ringing the bell. I went outside asked him what he wanted. He said he came to get his sister. I said she's your sister but she my wife now. Let me show you our license. He said I'm going to punch your lights out. I said to him take your best shot and get ready to go to jail. You know I wear glasses, you're not supposed to hit anybody who wears glasses. I told him are you going to do this or are you a plain chicken. Has he was leaving I said don't forget to bring your sister's clothes.

Make sure you bring them now, not tomorrow. He said he will tell his girlfriend. His girlfriend said I'll give them to you tomorrow. I said make sure. The next day his girlfriend threw them from the window. I said thanks. And I put them in the trash. I told his girlfriend I change my mind, I'll go and buy new clothes for my wife you can get these out of trash if you need them. I went back into the house. Later I went to JC Penney in Valley Stream, in Long Island. Purchase some clothes for my wife. Then stop at a news stand and purchased some newspapers looking for a new job. I see this ad, there an opening at N.Y.C.T.A. I apply for that job with N.Y.C.T.A. Looking for an electrical job. They had an opening as a coin corrected. I didn't want that job. Then I see in other paper there an opening in an electric department. I had to take a test. I took an electrical test. After two Weeks, I got a notice in mail. Report to Jay Street in Brooklyn. For an interview. I went to 370 Jay Street. In Brooklyn. Had an interview with personal department they told me to report the next day to 239th Street IRT shop in the Bronx. Starter this new job. On my birthday March 24.

In March of 1969 worked at different shops for 20 years. I retired in July 1989. I was placed in the Bronx as a car inspector. Working out of title. I spent six months there. Doing repairs, on I. R. T. trains.

Then I went to 207th Street main shop. I was now in Cars and Shops as a CME which is my title. THIS IS I.N.D. shop. My first department was the motor shop. Then I transfer to I.R.T. running repair shop. I took a few days off.

Then I went In December of 1969 flew to Puerto Rico. To meet Nancy's family, her mom, and her dad. Also her four brothers, and four sisters. All her nieces, and nephews. Her father took me out to meet all his friends and other people to have a drink. To celebrate, that he had a new son in law. Every place we stop his friends gave us a drink.

We was walking up the hill drunk. We stood another day. Then we flew back home. After we return back home. We flew on Pan America the ticket was one hundred dollar round trip, Friday till Sunday night. I had by brother in law pick us up from Kenney Airport. I went to Jamaica Shop to work as a maintenance electrical man. I maintain the shop. I work on 600 voltage D.C. I change out bulbs around shop. I also repaired power connectors that car inspectors used. To put six hundred volt to the car they was working on. Made up electrical bugs, this is a connector that goes into snake switch box. Replaced overhead power rails. Install portable a/c units into windows of offices. Install outlets in kitchen for cooks. Also ate breakfast there. I had to bump a man to be junior to me for me to get this job. This location was closed to where I lived.

Starting A Family

We flew again in October of 1970 to show her family our new born son. Born in July 1970. We had our son Baptist in August 1970. My sister and brother- in-law was God Parents. I problem the Priest we would come another day to get married in the Catholic Church. I told the priest we eloped to Elkton Maryland in November 1968. Her family was very happy she became a mother. They wish us the best. I went out with her dad again, He wanted to show me to all his friends again. Telling them I have a newborn son. And he had another grandson who lived in Brooklyn, New York. And had some more drinks. We came home drunk, again, but we had a great time. We flew back home. The next day. We rented a taxi, from Kenney Airport. When we got home we went to sleep.

In May of 1971 we got married again, this time in Saint Joseph Catholic Church. In May of 1974, we purchase a two family house in Richmond Hill, in Queens. New York. Fixed up basement so, my mom and dad can come and lived with us. And not lived in my sister and brother in law, Apartment any more. On August 10th 1974 my wife gave birth to our first daughter. She weight seven pounds two ounces.

In February 1976 purchased a piece of property in PA. In a small town outside of Newfoundland. It was a summer place in the Pocono Mountains. We would spend weekends there. All summer long. I would drive up Friday morning after worked till Monday night. I worked an eleven pm until seven am. I had Sundays and Mondays off. We Left our summer place around 6pm. Then drove back home into Queens. We spent vacations there also. I would take a vacation for a week at a time. I got four weeks in a year.

During July and August. Every third week I would take a week off on vacation. I would drive to our summer place. In the Pocono Mountains. Stay there a week, return home Monday afternoon, leave our car with Nancy and children. We got to meet other familiars. Also met an older couple. Fred and Peggy. They was from Chamber, PA we became very good friends. Fred and Peggy came up to the mountains. Every Friday night. If we was there they would stay until we left to go home.

I would take the Greyhound bus to Manhattan, then take train into Queens. Then walk home. Then go back to work Monday night to start work at 11pm till 7am. Then do this again the next week. On Friday morning I would take the train to Penn Station to get a grey hound bus to Scranton PA. My wife would pick me up, our children would stay with Fred and Peggy. In 1976. Our daughter fell down the stairs she was playing with my mom. Her grandma. My mom told her to come down the stairs. To play. But our daughter legs was too short. So our daughter fell down the steps. I took our daughter to the hospital to get checked out.

The hospital said they needed to keep our daughter overnight. My wife stood with her. I went home two see how my mother was. I found my mother laying on the steps. I called the police, they contact the hospital. The police call the eremangy service department. They call the ambulances and took my mother, to the Hospital. The hospital was Saint Marys. They was locater in Jamaica Queens, New York. My Nancy stood at hospital. With our daughter. I went to Saint Mary's to check on my mom. I found her in an intensive care unit. The police asked me what happen I explained to them. Told them my wife is at hospital with our daughter.

My daughter was released from hospital. The hospital took X-rays, found our daughter had a small fracture on her head. The stairs are wood, but the floor is concrete. We came back home. Got a neighbor to watch our son and daughter. My wife and I went to hospital to see how my mom was doing. They told us she is in the intensive unit. She had a Mimi stroke at the hospital, also had a Mimi stroke on the way to hospital. The nurse said she in bad shape. We're not allowed to go in the room now.

So we drove back home. I call the hospital the next day. They said we can come to see her now, because they don't think she going to live long. We call the neighbor again told her we needed her to watch our son and daughter. We need to go back to Saint Mary's hospital, can she come over. She said she would be right over. The neighbor came and we left, we got to hospital, and the nurse said she was sorry, my mom died a half hour ago. We went back home. Told our neighbor thank you. She said we should call her any time.

We went to visit my dad, later that day. We asked our neighbor if she can come by to watch our children. We need to go visit my dad again. He was at Far Rockaway Nursing Home. My dad asked where his wife was. I told him she was at home. After my third visit to see my dad. My dad kept asking where his wife is. I told him she wasn't feeling good. A few days later we went to visit dad again. Again he asked for mom. Again I said she has a cold. He kept asking where his wife is now.

I never found a way to tell him she died. He said to me he knows something is wrong. I said yes your right, mom died a few weeks ago. I didn't know how to tell you. You guys been together a long time. He told me to get the hell out. I left and went home. The next day the nursing home called me. Told me my dad died.

I went back to talk with them. To find out what I needed to do. They said they would take care of everything. They will call Pine Lawn because he's a vet and Have his body transfer there. First they will have a ceremony service at

Far Rockaway Church. In Far Rockaway. I told them to donate his belonging to others at the nursing home that might need some cloths. Also give his TV to someone. They said they will do as I wish.

I said to my wife, we need to rent the second floor apartment. We need to call a broker. The broker asked me if I ever thought about selling this house. I told him no He said to me if I ever. How much would I want? So I figure I purchase this house in 1974 this was 1984. I figure property went up three thousand a year. I have this house ten years. I said about sixthly six thousand. When I purchased this house I paid thirty two thousand six hundred. I bought it for Sixty Two thousand. He said he could get us eighty-four thousand. I told him I would think about it. I'll call him when we came home from vacation. While we was at the Pocono Mountains I and my Nancy spoke about the selling of the house. And buying a bigger house. Because we needed more space. I called him, told him we decided to sell.

We needed to find a larger house. We look at and purchase a one family home in Wakefield in Queens. New York. I took my wife and daughter to Rosenberg Hospital in Queens. Have them check out my daughter. Again our daughter was complaining that her head was hurting. They checked her out, they said it was a normal head ache, she might have hit her head some where they couldn't find anything. Wrong. While a few months later. In October my wife gave birth to our second daughter. After second daughter born. October 17.

My wife indicated she want to go back to worked. When our daughter, get older. When our daughter became about five years old. My wife wanted to look for that job. She was talking about. She seen a job opening at Kennedy Airport. She went there for an interview. They hire her. She took that job it started at 8pm until midnight, she work at Kennedy Airport. AS a British Airliner plane cleaner. Cleaning inside planes. She started this job in 1984. She left that job in March of 1989.

She hurt her knee on a plane. She was walking up the stairs. The cleaner and other staff members used the outside stairs platform. There not allowed to go through the inside of terminal. This is the company rule. Someone spill something on the plat form. My wife didn't see anything. Step on platform and slip into side of plane. This was in November. Of banging her left knee. They sent her for X-rays. She had torn ligament. She had to have some surgery on her knee. I was going to retired. In July of 1989. I Retired in July of 1989. From N.Y.C.T.A. In 1988 went on vacation, made a trip to Florida. Went around looking at homes. Wanted to see what the prices of home was. Look at a few houses the broker showed us about six or seven properties.

Then indicated he had a foreclosure that He got in a week ago. He told us about this foreclosure every time he show us a property. He then said he was going to show us the property we came to see. That property was on five areas it was a prefabricator home. It was selling for Fifth-Nine thousand. Then he said if you guys want I can stop at this foreclosure. I said yes let shop and look.

I THROUGH MAYBE THERE SOMETHING I NEED TO SEE. We stop but he didn't have the key. He said he's going to drive us back to his office. We got back to his office. He handed me the key. He said we should drive back and look at this property inside. He said this property is listed for seventh nine thousand we stop to see it. But he didn't have the key. He said he need to go back to his office. We look around the property. He then drove back to his office. Then he handed me the key. He said after you see the inside and around the outside.

Then come by in morning let him know what we think. So we drove back to property. This was a block house. We look inside and out. We notice it needed work on outside and inside. We went back to his office the next morning. Before going back to hotel we stop at local store and purchase a couple of newspapers, to see what homes are selling for. This house had 3 bedrooms, possible 4th. Plus two bathrooms. The local paper indicated that 3 bedroom 2 bath was selling for$ 79,999. We couldn't afford another 80,000.00. House. So when we got back to hotel. We talk together about this house.

Return to his office. We told him, we couldn't afford that house. He told us to make an offer. He would send it to the bank. First thing this afternoon. So we offer him $ 57,000.00 with $ 7000.00 down. I gave the broker a hand shake, and told him if everything goes good. I'll send him a check of $ 7000.00. We will try to purchase this block house on almost 2 acres of land.

In September of 1988, I drove down with my son. I needed to go to closing. We was able and did purchased this house. After I retired in 1989 moved with family to Florida. Moved with wife, and 2 daughters. Our son stood with his uncle and my sister. He was working at a bank in Long Island as a bank teller accounting. He was working at night. He work from five pm until nine pm counting money placed in outside vault. My sister and brother- in law said it was o.k. with them. So on August 31 we drove to Florida.

Florida

We arrived at our new home on September 1, 1989. We unpack truck, Put everything inside house. Put beds together. Now we was able to sleep. The following morning we took the truck back to Penske. My wife drove our car behind me. I gave back the truck. The sales person asked me how much I paid to rent this truck in New York. I told him what I paid. One thousand two hundred dollars. He said to me I could have come to Florida rented a truck there. Drove it to New York and drove it back to Florida, then bring it to them and save money. And save a lot of money. I told him I never knew or through about doing something like that it cost me Nine hundred thirty dollars. Plus I had to pay extra for gas. Drove back home. Started to clean inside. The house. Removed old green carpet from first living room floor. Purchased stick on tiles. Laid down tiles. Build a wall by extra room at side entrance of house made a room to store some others items. Made other repairs inside. Put up new curtain in all rooms. Also clean all windows. We have thirteen windows.

Made repairs to outside of house. Repaired soffit around house. Purchased two by six by ten studs to replaced rotten studs. Call a contractor to install. Aluminum siding over two by six on soffit. House came with an in ground pool. Had to buy in ground liner. Went to Pinch and Penny. Pinch and Penny is a pool supply store. To purchased liner. Made some other repairs inside house removed carpet from other living room replaced with stick on tiles there to. This house had two living rooms. Had to get a well pump. To supply water to house. Purchase a well pump from Lowes Also started looking for work.

Had a friend help me put a new roof on house. Had a contractor install a new Air/conditioner for house. Had a contractor install a car port on end of house. Took a job at UF. In an electric company, Yulee was company name. Worked there for six months. Got laid off, this was an OPS job. Started looking for another job. Then took a job working in a nursing home. Repairing wheel chairs, maintaining building. Cleaning wheel chairs. Doing electrical and plumbing repairs. Work with another fellow. Worked there about a year. This other fellow wanted to be a supervisor, When Dan the superintended went on vacation. This fellow went to the head of nursing.

He had her made him head of maintenance. Because she was the one to had him come in for this job? After Dan came back from his vacation. He call me into his office. He told me he made the other fellow head of maintenance. I said to him before you went on vacation you was talking to me about getting rid of this other fellow. Because you heard he wasn't doing is job. He said to me are you mad. I said no. I'll be looking for a new job soon. I don't like to be stab in the back. This nursing home was Gainesville Nursing Home. I'm not going to do all the work around here for him to look good. I started looking for jobs in local papers. I quite this job. After I got another job. I took a job at an apartment complex. Doing maintenance. Repairing electrical, plumbing. Making keys. Picking grounds after about a year I left. This apartment complex. The name was Country Garden Apartment in Gainesville.

For more money took another Maintenance job. For more money. Learn air-condition. Got certify, worked there for a few months. Left there for more money.

Took another job as a Maintenance helper, the supervisor went on vacation and never return. The maintenance department Director came by to see how things are going. I asked him how does someone applies for a supervisor position. He then said He made me the supervisor. Then I became the supervisor. Worked at this job for 3 years. Doing repairs to electrical and plumbing and glass. Also working at a sister property. Doing repairs there as well.

Then took another job as a Maintenance manager. Doing repairs to electric, plumbing, air condition and heating. Making keys, changing locks. Had two people under me. This was Hidden Lake Apartment. Worked there for four years two months. They change Property managers. This guy Mike took over. After four months he was there he didn't like me because I was making more money. I left there. I went to another retirement housing apartment building. Making Repairs to electric, changing light bulbs, changing air condition filters. Trouble shooting air conditions and heating problems. Installing new lighting. Troubled shooting A/C and heating systems. Working in the kitchen trouble shooting appliance. Installing new a/c wall units. Picking up supply at supply companies. Then taking them too different. Departments. Then I got sick.

Had wife take me to North Florida Hospital emergency room. I was checked from head to toe. X-ray was taken. White cells was very high. Red cells was low. Emergency doctor said I had Arthritis. He said I needed to go to an Arthritis doctor. The Arthritis doctor treated me with Arthritis medicine that didn't help. I was put on a steroid. We started with 15 mg. Increase five mg per day. Then went to 60 mg a day. The pain was gone. The Arthritis doctor told me I need to come off the medicine, it's no good for my body.

I asked him why he gave it to me. He said he had to find something to get rid of my pain. I Tried coming off of steroid. I came off to fast. I had to go back on. When all pain was gone. I stop taking this medicine. A few days later, pain came back. I went back to doctor this second time around put me back on steroid with Actonel. If doctor gave me Actonel the first time. Actonel helps to prevent bone loss. If the doctor gave me the Actonel the first time. I would have been better. I would still have my left knee. I couldn't walk, I had to drag my left leg.

I went to see Dr Parr, he sent me to Dr. Lane. Dr Lane gave me three choses. First made a special brace, it would cost Six thousand dollars. I told him I don't have any money, but give me day or so I would contacted my union. See what they can justness. Or I can get half the knee replaced. Or last option is replaced the whole knee. If I do half of knee. I might have to do other half later.

So I agree to do whole knee. I had to have my left knee replaced. I had left knee replaced in February, 2008. In March of 2008 went back to North Florida Hospital with bad stomach pains. Met the right doctor. He said I had Lymphoma. I asked what Lymphoma was. He said its cancer. I asked if there a treatment for this. He said I needed to check into the hospital He would come by first thing in morning. I checked myself in. He said he was right. I had Lymphoma Non- Hopkins stage 3. He said he was sending me down stairs. The hospital will install a port in my chest. Then tomorrow they will give me a dose of chemo. If everything goes right, I will be discharge at end of week. I will then come to see him at his office in two weeks. He will set me up with a plan. I went to his office, he set me up with five more chemo.

Sick

I came down with non- Hopkins Lymphoma stage 3. In 2008 I became disabled for six years. Every fiv weeks I went for chemo. I had five chemo. My lymphoma went into remission. My wife had a Mimi stroke in 2005. Her Mimi stroke kept her from driving. Her emotion made her body turn to the right. In 2008 I took her to see Dr. Pickens. She had a lump on her back. Later she found out this lump was cancer. Breast Cancer stage 4. In 2009. She had Pain in her back, the family doctor we had gave her a shot of condone. I went to the cancer doctor at his office. He told me he would treat me with five more chemo. He would give me chemo every three weeks. After 6 years. I was placed on retirement with Social Security. I was taken out of disability. My wife was still fighting with her breast cancer stage 4. I went back out looking for a job. Took a job with home depot. In 2013 worked there for 3 years. Worked in electrical department, also in plumbing. Our youngest daughter was taking her mother (my wife) to doctors. While I was working. I quit home depot in 2016. I met a painter that I hired when I was a maintenance supervisor at Hidden Lake Apartment complex. He asked me if I remembered Jan. I told him yes. He then gave me her phone number and where she was working. He told me she needs an assistant supervisor. He told me to call her. I did, she told me to come and see her. I made an appointment. I visit her, we talk for a while. She said she is hiring me. She introduced me to the supervisor. I went to have a drug test. It was nine weeks later.

That they told me to come in to start work. I was working at this apartment complex where I twisted my knee, a few days later they fired me. A couple of days later. They indicated I was going into apartments without indicating who I was, this isn't true, and they never got me any uniforms. I would knock on the doors. Three times. I didn't get any answer I open the door a little and loud in saying this is maintenance. If I didn't get an answer. I would go inside to do my repairs. A couple of times after a few minutes a man came out of back room. He asked me what I was doing, I said I'm here to check out your dish washer. He said shouldn't I have a company shirt or uniform. I said yes but I haven't got any. Two days later I was fired. They indicated I can go to the Care center for treatment of my knee. Which I did. I went to a knee doctor, he said I should have my knee replace, but I didn't.

I got a part time job. At a nursing home. My wife is still fighting her breast cancer Stage 4, I decided to Quit. In September of 2020. I went with my wife to her cancer doctor. He indicated he needed to get her a new chemo pill, I then retired. Start going with wife to all her doctors and taking care of her, instead of working. I went with my wife in October, the doctor indicated. That her scans was great, no problems. He never got her chemo. In November I took my wife to doctor, he asked, he doesn't see scan documents. My wife told him he or his office staff didn't send the referral. To Invision. He said he was going to send them now. She asked him about her chemo In December 2020 she had a CT on Dec. 16 and a bone scan on Dec 21. Went to Dr. Balamucki. on January 2. He showed us both scans. The CT showed cancer is at her Liver, and her brain. Bone scan, showed cancer all over her bones. Took her to cancer Doctor on January sixth. He said my wife is going too died. I said what you are talking about. He said he never seen the cancer spread so fast. He doesn't know why. This was a big lie.

In January of 2021, the Cancer WON. My wife Died on the 24th. This is the doctor faith. He admitted it to me, he forgot to order the new chemo pills. He should have order these pills in September 2020. But he didn't. He should have ordered them in. October 2020. But he again he forgot. I went to see him on May 11. At 9 am. I had an appointment for him to check my Lymphoma. I asked him if he knew now, why the cancer spread so fast in my wife, he said no. I asked him if he can check her records. I text him on May 13. At 9.02 am. I asked him if he found anything. He said she was too weak. I asked when she was too weak. He indicated at the end of 2020. I asked what month. He said he would text me later. Also I text him on May 14. At 3.22 He called be back on May 14 at 3:39 pm. I was trying to text him, but I must have hit the phone button instance. He was waiting for my call. This is when he told me he forgot to order my wife chemo pills. They was not pills, it was an injection. He didn't get or give her this chemo, becaused she could die in is office. How would he explained this.

Family

Our son still resided in Big Apple. Lives in Queens with wife and one son. He is an Electronic Engineer. His wife is an Airline Stewardess. Their son is in High School.

Our oldest daughter resided in Florida. Lives in Lake Butler. With husband and 2 sons. She is a teacher. Her husband is an Engineer. Oldest son works in Hospital. Youngest son in High School.

Our youngest daughter resided in Lake Butler, Florida. With her husband and her three daughters. This daughter is a nurse. Her husband works in Maintenance. Oldest daughter works as an Art designer. Second daughter works part time as a lab tech. Her youngest daughter is in High School.

Sick Again

With the death of wife. I became very unhappy, sad, and very emotional. Had to go to family doctor, to get help. He gave me Alprazolam 0.25 mg. told me to take Alprazolam. When my emotion get unstable. Later he gave me Escitalopram 10 mg. This should help me more than the Alprazolam. In 2020 I was going to get a Tattoo, but I didn't. April 5, 2021. I went and got a tattoo. The cancer ribbon, half green and half pink. Had our names placed in green and pink side of ribbon? Had this tattoo placed 1" lower then elbow? Want everyone to see it. My wife was everything to me. I miss her dearly. I loved her then and now and forever. I'm planning to have another tattoo put on right arm one inch below elbow. This one is going to be a heart with a lady bug inside and two names. Hope and Brooklyn Bob.

Today - The Present

Looking back at the pass
We just celebrated 2022
January 1, New Year's Day

'm looking back at yesterday. I celebrated New Years with family, but not my wife. She died almost a year ago. She died of Breast Cancer stage # 4, on the 24th, of January 2021. I also missed her for Christmas, and Thanksgiving. Her Birthday and our Anniversary, both days in November. The 12 Th, and 23rd I'm very lonely without her. I know her in a better place. No pain and suffering. I'm the one who has the pain and emptiness.

She was my first loved and will only be. There will not be another. When someone died it hurts, but when your loved one died the world get empty. She died due to doctor's negligence. Attorneys can't help, because Florida Laws won't let them. Florida law lets doctors get away with murdering people that have Breast Cancer. This doctor was giving my wife large milligrams chemo pills. This cause her heart to enlarge. When her heart got enlarge, he stop giving her chemo. Because he didn't want her to die in his office. How would he explain this to authorities? He couldn't.

In May of 2021. I had an appointment with this doctor for my Lymphoma. He checked me out, said I was looking good. He would make another appointment for May of 2022. I said that's good. I asked him why the cancer spread so fast in my wife. He said he didn't know. I asked him if he could check her records. Two days later he called me back, said he forgot to get her or give her chemo. This was a big lie. I have proof. My wife's medical records.

We fell in loved in 1968. We married in November. We been married for over 52 years. We had our ups and downs. But we stood together. Blood is thicker than water. We forth a little, but making up was great. We had four children, but the first died before being born. He was a boy. So we raise one son and two daughters. Son lives in the Big Apple, our two daughters lived here in the orange.

I know that people who have or had cancer, there life is shorten, all depends on type of cancer, or how hard they fight to live. How strong they are. Breast cancer is a number one killer. I have Lymphoma, it's in remission for fourteen years. I never realize just how many people have cancer. Until I went for chemo.

I always think how people feel when they know that their going to die. My wife knew her whose going to die, even before the doctor told her. She had a lot of pain, but never would say. I could feel it. In my heart. I believed if the doctor said she had enlarge heart, our family doctor would have told the heart specialist. But he never said anything. But the cancer doctor didn't want anyone to know he did negligence.

For our 53rd Anniversary, I gave my wife a figurine of griffin's neck twisting. Nana & Papa. Plus yellow roses, in my mind they was Gold. For her Birthday I gave her a Swan figurine with associated flowers. Also 3 small swans, with our children names. Placed this on the dining room table.

Yesterday to Present

As of January 24, 2021.

My wife died of her Breast Cancer Stage 4. My life has change very much. I know, but I believed it's my fault. I wasn't there for her a 100%.

I loved her then, now, and always. Forever until I died and later when we meet again. Hopefully.

I get these second images. From nowhere. I'll see her in her death bed. This takes me back till the day one. When I found her death. I remember that day. It was January 24, 2021. I was sleeping on the sofa. I got up to pee. I came back to the sofa, as I passed her bed. She was sleeping in a hospital bed in living room. I glance at her, her eyes was sleety open. I sat back on sofa, just then GOD told me to check her, I got up went back over to her. I took my right hand, placed it on her right arm. Her arm was ice cold, I then took my hand place it on her chest, there was no movement. Then took my hand placed it by her nose, there was no air. She was death. The time was 6 am.

Another time was. I took my granddaughter to Kay jewelry. My wife told her and her two other sister. To take something from her jewelry box. To remember her. This was in December of 2020. Our middle aged granddaughter took a black onyx ring. I took it to Kay Jeweler to get it size down. Two weeks later, Kay jewelry called it was ready to be pick up. I said to my granddaughter lets go. Go with me, so you can try it on to be sure it fit. After she put it on her thump. I took her to buffalo wing. To have some lunch. After we ordered some wings and drinks. My granddaughter took my two arms. I said are you ok? She said to me. Am I ok I said yes why! She said I had a sad look on my face. I told her it was that picture hanging at Kay's. A young couple holding hands, it remind me of your nana and me when we was young. This day was a Wednesday. The day the doctor told me my wife is going to die. This was January 6, 2021.

Another time I went with my daughter, and youngest granddaughter to the photo shop, my granddaughter had to take a photo for her school. My granddaughter asked if we can stop and get some Mexican food, I said yes. So we stop at this new placed in Gainesville. We all ordered different foods. When the food came, I couldn't eat. My lovely wife was from Puerto Rico. She wasn't there so I couldn't eat. I ate the Mexican food around 10 pm that night. At the table near my wife picture and ashes. I told her I miss her a lot, I wish she was here.

I never knew or though I would miss her. I love her very, very much. I also had moments.   In May, on Mother's Day. My daughter and I purchased mother day balloon. We got 13 balloons, we gave one balloon to each of my granddaughter, her daughters. We went outside. We had them let the balloon go. They flew into heaven. So there nana would see them. Then we all took another

40

balloon and let it go into heaven again. Together this time. There was many different things that took place. I left one balloon in the house. Which said I Love You.

My son came down with his son and dog. He spent nine days. Help me redo the kitchen. We change some of the cabinets. The sink cabinet, this one was falling apart. Then we placed tiles on the wall. Behind the range, on side of wall above countertop. Along sink cabinet, into, near wall of washer room. Down to floor. After he left to go home. I had to buy more tiles. For that area to finish. I had to clean the whole house. I purchased some new ornaments. Cardinal wind chime. I placed them in the car port. Some cardinal curtains for the kitchen window. Also purchased hanging solar angels. I put them in our Memorial Garden. I cleaned up the garden, removed some weeds that came through the mulch. I took more yellow ribbon, placed it around a palm tree near the car port. I trim around the front of our house.

On Father's Day. I purchased six balloon. These balloon was miss you and love you. We all had one balloon. We let these balloon go at the same time, into heaven. We stood there until we couldn't see the balloons any more. They floated into the sky. On July 4th, I purchased firecracker. We fired them off at midnight, and said a pray.

On Labor Day. We got together outside and said a prayed to my wife, mother, and nana.

October 20, 2021. I went to Oasis, Had Paul put a Plane tattoo on my arm. It's a plane, which as the sun picture on tail wing. With PR in middle. Below wing is a motor. In my mind this plane is a D C 10. The ones we took to fly to Puerto Rico. In the seventh's. On the motor it has 11-1968. This stand for November 1968. This is when we got married. Next to this is an apple, which stands for New York. Next is Bklyn, Which is Brooklyn where we met. Next to that is a bridge, on other side of bridge is an orange, which stands for Florida. So this tattoo, is a sign for. We met in Brooklyn NY. Lived there for twenty years. Then moved to Florida.

I'm thinking if I do another tattoo. It will be, Nov. 1968 until Jan. 2021.

November 12th. I purchased six balloons. They was Miss and Love you. One for each of us. We let them go at 10 am, the time my wife and I got married in 1968.

November 23rd. I purchased ten balloon. All Happy Birthday. My son and his family drove down from the apple for Thanksgiving. We all let the balloon fly into the sky into heaven. At six pm, after dinner. I also had special balloon made. Your first year in Heaven. I also order one balloon for Christmas in Heaven. I'll pick it up on December 23rd.

December 24th. I purchase eighteen balloon. Six Merry Christmas, and six Miss you, and six Love you.

Printed in the United States
by Baker & Taylor Publisher Services